# can't **lose**

## a self-encouragement book

### Dr. Anthony J. Perkins

**author**HOUSE®

*AuthorHouse™*
*1663 Liberty Drive*
*Bloomington, IN 47403*
*www.authorhouse.com*
*Phone: 1 (800) 839-8640*

*Published by AuthorHouse  04/07/2020*

*ISBN: 978-1-7283-5807-9 (sc)*
*ISBN: 978-1-7283-5806-2 (e)*

# Contents

# A Note to the Reader

This work is designed as a self-encouragement book. It embraces 21 qualities you can reflect on and use to inspire your daily life. As you engage with this book, you are encouraged to take inventory of your thoughts and put them into action. How you choose to apply these qualities can motivate you every day.

# Prayer

God, assist readers to understand that their attitude affects what they see, think, and do. Help them to believe that they *can't lose* when they truly practice these qualities at a high level. Utilize this book to increase their capacity and serve others. Amen.

# one

**SMILE**

## You can smile because . . .

You are alive
You have a beautiful life filled with blessings
You have the mindset to overcome obstacles
You have a strong support system
You love the animals in your life
You have a great career
You are healthy
You conquered a medical set-back
You serve others
You are intelligent
You are valuable
You teach others
Your journey in life inspires others
You do not maintain, you advance
You learn from others
You have a roof over your head
Your attitude is positive

Your smile is one of your most powerful assets. Strive every day to make smiling addictive; it yields a plethora of positive effects. Did you know that it takes more muscles to frown than it does to smile? Conserve energy by smiling!

All of us have some type of negativity in our lives. No matter how much we try to avoid pessimism, it can creep in. Pessimism might pertain to frustrations with traffic, people, or it might involve more profound challenges. I encourage you to smile even when things come against you. Remember that there are always others who have it worse. Sometimes what seems like a terrible thing can actually be for the best. Make it a habit every day to appreciate, smile, and live your beautiful life.

I am a person who exercises, eats on the healthy side most of the time, and makes every effort to embrace a positive lifestyle. Even so, in 2019, I was diagnosed with colon cancer. After two surgeries, two colonoscopies, and three months of chemotherapy, I went from being a hungry person in life to being the hungriest person on the planet.

What do I mean by being hungry? I mean giving back, serving others, achieving goals, being a better parent, increasing my capacity by learning, writing books, making inspirational videos, and appreciating life to its fullest. This experience was simultaneously difficult and amazing. I was blessed to beat colon cancer.

Remember, in this life, we are never promised a tomorrow. Take the time to feel the wind in your face, to appreciate the beauty of the mountains, clouds, and nature, and to adore your family. We have an unlimited number of things to smile about, yet we often focus on the negative elements of life. I encourage you to think of any negative situation as 10 seconds of your time. We are given 86,400 seconds in each day, so be okay with giving away those 10 seconds because you have 86,390 seconds of blessings, positivity, and beautiful moments remaining. Smile and know that today is now.

How can your smile contribute to others?
Please list examples below:

_____  _____

_____  _____

_____  _____

_____  _____

_____  _____

_____  _____

_____  _____

_____  _____

_____  _____

_____  _____

_____  _____

_____  _____

_____  _____

_____  _____

_____  _____

_____  _____

_____  _____

REFLECTIVE PAUSE

Listen to the tortoise
— use your smile to be
a better version of you.

# two

## RICHNESS

## You are rich with . . .

Support
Love
Knowledge
Family
Success
Life
Beauty
Strength
Purpose
Health
Fortitude
Comeback power
Mindfulness
Kindness
Service
Relationships
Rewards

Make every day the best day of your life. Think about it: on each new day, you are the youngest you will ever be. You are rich beyond belief. Outside of the material items, you are rich with life's little and big things. You are rich with love when your children are born, you are rich with knowledge when you learn, you are rich with expertise when you accomplish your goals, you are rich with determination when you overcome a setback, you are rich with memories when you have strong relationships, and you are rich with appreciation when you take in the beautiful moments of your life.

It is easy to get caught up in the negative minutiae of life. Why? Because there are many people and unlimited amounts of misleading information trying to steer you down the wrong path. At the end of this wrong path are defeat, ordinariness, and mediocrity. Many people stay on this path and never escape it.

There is a story I once heard that I want to share with you. There was a rich family that had everything. The father and his son of this rich family visited the home of the father's best friend, a man who was very poor. On the way home from the visit, the father reminded his son of how blessed they were as compared to the family they had just visited. The son replied that the family, while considered poor in a material sense, was rich with love, positive family relationships, respect, faith, honor, and tenacity. The father smiled and realized that this visit was a great teachable moment for them both. Richness in life is not about possessions. Your richness in life should be in exact proportion to the characteristics you demonstrate. The key to your richness rests in your mind.

How much richness do you want in your life? You can be as rich as you desire. It is a matter of ensuring richness is a part of your purpose. Do not imitate others, be genuine with all of your richness.

What characteristics will give you richness?
Please list examples below:

_____

_____

_____

_____

_____

_____

_____

_____

_____

_____

_____

_____

_____

_____

_____

_____

_____

_____

REFLECTIVE PAUSE

*Life is a blank canvas;
paint the richness you want.*

# three

## LEARNING

## Learning can . . .

Expand your mind
Promote your thinking
Bring you to new heights
Set you up for success
Separate you from the pack
Make you feel confident
Help you prepare others
Change your behavior
Motivate you
Offer you intellectual stimulation
Improve your focus
Give you direction
Add foundation to your principles
Give you credibility
Add to your progress
Give you results
Enhance you

Learning is in you. Learning will help you gain new substance and meaning in all that you do. Believe that you can learn in every moment so you can live to your greatest promise. "Learning" can be defined as the process of acquiring new—or modifying existing—knowledge, behaviors, skills, values, or preferences. Humans, animals, and even some machines possess the ability to learn.

Make learning a priority, and realize that you can always learn new things. Those who believe they know everything can never learn. No matter how many times you revisit a subject, problem, or activity, you can always learn one more thing. For instance, say you want to learn about overcoming depression; each time you research the topic, you will learn new information. Do not believe that once you have looked into something you know everything about it.

Use learning to teach others. Maya Angelou once stated, "When you learn, teach. When you get, give." Make learning a great experience for those around you. Life is about building your capacity and passing along your knowledge. Use your learning to make breakthroughs, cure diseases, and lead innovations.

You are more prepared than you think you are to start learning. Stop doubting and start doing. Use learning to shape your character, build your confidence, become more determined, do more, and exude resilience. Never stop learning, because learning enriches and expands you. Establish yourself by learning; make it a behavior, a habit, and a commitment. Use it as a stepping stone to take you higher. By changing your attitude to learn, you can change the course of your life. Use learning to bypass reasons and get results. We need you!

**R**
**E**
**F**
**L**
**E**
**C**
**T**
**I**
**V**
**E**

**P**
**A**
**U**
**S**
**E**

How can learning bring you to new heights?
Please list examples below:

_____
_____
_____
_____
_____
_____
_____
_____
_____
_____
_____
_____
_____
_____
_____
_____
_____
_____

When you learn, teach others
so that they can blossom.

# four

## LOVE

**Love of . . .**

Country
Self
Others
Career
Children
Life
Philanthropy
Education
Service
Giving back
Teaching
Family
Art
Animals
Music
Faith
Our planet

One of Howard Jones' hit songs is titled, "What Is Love?" That seems to be the million-dollar question today, in this era of quick divorces and dissatisfaction with relationships. Ask yourself these two questions when it comes to love:

Do you really understand what love entails?

Are you putting your best effort into your love?

Your answers to these questions will reveal the honest facts of where you are with love.

Love refers to a feeling of strong attraction and emotional attachment. Love of a hobby differs from love of children or a spouse. All of us have love within us and choose to distribute it in various ways. Some people show love physically, by touching and kissing; others do so by giving gifts or sharing kind words. What is your method?

As you reflect on this subject, consider this story. A man went to a counselor to discuss love and receive strategies for improvement. He did not realize that his visit would be a wisdom moment. The counselor began by stating, "I am sorry to hear you lost your wife in an accident." To which the man replied, "I did not lose my wife; she is alive and well, and I love her." The counselor continued with, "I am sorry you lost your house in a recent fire." But the man insisted, "I love my beautiful home, and I did not lose it in a fire." The counselor then offered, "I am sorry you lost your career in those recent layoffs." And yet the man assured him, "I love my career, and I did not lose it. There were no layoffs." The man then realized the counselor's point: when times are tough and you think you lost that loving feeling, remember, love is all around us. It never leaves us; we just need to press that reset button in our mind. You are reading this book for a reason. Ask yourself: Can I do better with my love? Whatever situation you are in, reflect on it and then insert the power of love. Remember the lyric from the Beatles song from decades ago: "All you need is love."

**R E F L E C T I V E   P A U S E**

How can you enhance your love?
Please list examples below:

_____
_____
_____
_____
_____
_____
_____
_____
_____
_____
_____
_____
_____
_____
_____
_____
_____
_____
_____
_____
_____

*In your busy life, starve your
distractions and feed your love.*

# five

## YOU DESERVE

**You deserve . . .**

Respect
A chance
An opportunity
Love
To advance
To use your gifts
Joy
Achievement
Favor
Great health
Happiness
Promotion
Great relationships
Growth
To shine
To transform
To evolve

Please be cautious of the "deserving" attitude. If you allow your ego to take over, "you deserve" can turn into a bad thing. If you use "you deserve" in a humble manner, or as something to strive for, the words can be rewarding. It is best to approach "you deserve" with modest grace. I always tell students, "If you make positive choices and put an effort behind those choices, your 'you deserve' moments will be plentiful."

As humans, sometimes we have a tendency to go overboard with "you deserve." Because you work hard, "you deserve" can become a weekend trip to the mall where you exceed your budget and go into debt. Because you passed a class, "you deserve" can turn into a celebration where you overconsume food or drink. Because you had a baby, "you deserve" can lead you to spoil your child instead of finding the proper balance between yes and no. These examples are evidence of how "you deserve" can go wrong.

You deserve great things, but are you going to handle "you deserve" in a down-to-earth fashion and with proper planning? A big part of preserving momentum in your life involves your responses to challenges. Are you going to be cocky or meek in your "you deserve" approach?

The relationship between the bow and arrow is a great example for this topic. In order for an arrow to be launched forward, it must first be pulled back. This movement often parallels our own lives, as we, too, must go backwards to move forward. Be careful in assuming that moving forward is the only direction in life, because going backwards is also part of your journey. Yes, you deserve the best, but you must also be realistic. Ensure and believe that you have all the prerequisites in life to handle the responsibility of "you deserve."

How can you help others with
their "you deserve?"
Please list examples below:

_____
_____
_____
_____
_____
_____
_____
_____
_____
_____
_____
_____
_____
_____
_____
_____
_____
_____
_____
_____
_____

REFLECTIVE PAUSE

You are enough; you deserve to go out and conquer your world.

# six
## ADVERSITY

## Adversity is an opportunity . . .

For heroism
To learn
To overcome
To stand out
To bring out your best
To seize the moment
To zoom out and gain perspective
To discover your brilliant body of work
To break that nerve and accomplish things
To establish your path
To move forward and take someone with you
To conduct yourself with dignity and tenaciousness
To have good thoughts, say good
words, and do good deeds
To show your grit
To breakthrough
To keep fear in check
To kick butt

Never let adversity define you in a negative way. Always view it in a positive light and treat it as an opportunity. People will try to judge you by the adversity you face. Flip the script and beat them to the punch by conquering it with class. Admit there was a situation, gather the appropriate people, create a plan, and triumph over your adversity. Use it as a learning experience, and consider it a blessing in disguise.

Imagine you are a baseball player who hits a homerun every time you get up to bat. Because of your great talent, you might stop practicing. As funny as it may seem, baseball players, like anyone else, must face hardships, such as striking out, in order to keep striving for more—in order to stay hungry.

Always look for ways to use adversity to your advantage. There are many people who have, for example, lost a loved one but who have used the experience to establish an annual scholarship or who have raised funds to battle diseases. They turned their adversity into a focus; they found a silver lining and realized purpose in their adversity.

You have a unique assignment in life. When it is disrupted with misfortune, instead of complaining, jump into solution mode. When adversity comes along, do not go with it. Consider asking and answering these questions when you are in an adverse situation:

- ✓ How will I overcome this adversity in a calm manner?
- ✓ How can I rise to greatness with this adversity?
- ✓ What is my vision to make this adversity a teachable moment?

- ✓ How can I make each second count when overcoming this adversity?
- ✓ How can I use the abilities of my teammates or family when I face adversity?
- ✓ Can I include faith to get me/us through this adversity?

How can you use adversity to
bring out the best in you?
Please list examples below:

_____
_____
_____
_____
_____
_____
_____
_____
_____
_____
_____
_____
_____
_____
_____
_____
_____
_____

REFLECTIVE PAUSE

*When it comes to adversity,*
*know that you have got this.*
*Then, celebrate your victory.*

# seven

## WHO SAID YOU COULD NOT?

## WHO SAID YOU COULD NOT...

Get out of debt?
Manage your anxiety?
Accomplish your dreams?
Complete those courses?
Raise your children?
Stop temptations?
Handle failure?
Find solutions?
Be a person of excellence?
Have a family?
Be disciplined?
Be a role model?
Leave a positive legacy?
Change lives?
Be a difference maker?
Do right with your time on Earth?
Win your battles?

Never let anyone make a big decision for you unless you are a youngster or you really need someone's experienced advice. Imagine standing in front of a judge who is about to make a decision regarding your future. Is this truly the position you want to be in? It is best that YOU make your own decisions in regards to your future. Your vision, focus, and direction in life are forged by your thinking, actions, and drive to succeed.

How often have you heard stories of people overcoming obstacles, breaking barriers, or succeeding with few resources? The answer is, countless times. Make a promise to yourself to disregard doubt and fear. You will be cognizant of these feelings, but do not allow them to occupy your mind. Outsmart them by stating positive affirmations and by refreshing your mind with optimism. Never forget what you were able to achieve when it seemed like "game over" for you.

Not too long ago, I called a mechanic because my car was due for an oil change. He said he could not provide the service, because he did not have an oil filter in stock for my car. I politely requested that he either order an appropriate filter or call another store to locate one, while also reminding him that I had been in for this service three months before. He stated that they would no longer special order parts or request them from other stores.

I was shocked by this response, because my request had been fairly standard and reasonable. What kind of business does not provide such basic customer service? What I asked for was not impossible. And what is next: Those in need of a heart replacement must bring in their own heart prior to surgery? This oil mechanic is obviously a "can't" person. Do not let "can't" people into your life unless they are *can't lose* people. Incorporate and operate under a "can" boldness.

A "can" assertiveness means being more determined than others, and a "can" outlook begins with certainty. I once heard that if you want something, ask for it. If you do not get it, take it—take it in an appropriate manner, take it with courage, and take it with passion. I ended up driving to that business a few days later to speak with the manager, and guess what: The shop ordered a filter and, a few days later, completed my oil change. As the late great ESPN host Stuart Scott used to say, "Boo-yah!"

How can you overcome. . .who
said you could not?
Please list examples below:

_____

_____

_____

_____

_____

_____

_____

_____

_____

_____

_____

_____

_____

_____

_____

_____

R
E
F
L
E
C
T
I
V
E
P
A
U
S
E

*Stop talking, branch out, and show them.*

# eight
**EXTRAORDINARY**

**Transform from ordinary to
always extraordinary by . . .**

Learning

Volunteering

Sharing your knowledge

Touching lives

Eliminating regrets

Understanding good enough
no longer works for you

Giving it your all

Knowing things will come sooner than expected

Having more energy than the problem

Including God in your life

Creating

Having a positive attitude

Rewarding others

Living better

Being active

Thinking smarter

Eating healthier

Yₒu can talk yourself into or out of extraordinary. Ask yourself this: Do you want ordinary food at a restaurant or extraordinary food? Do you want to raise ordinary children or extraordinary children? Do you want an ordinary education or an extraordinary education? I am sure that your answer to all three questions was "extraordinary," so why put up with "ordinary" in so many arenas of life?

How do you go from someone who regularly settles for ordinary to someone who always strives for extraordinary? Take the example of a high-performance car. For a vehicle to execute at its highest level, the owner needs to use the best oil, gas, and tires, and also needs to get regular tune-ups by the best mechanic.

This same notion should govern your attitude. To be extraordinary is to be disciplined in your thinking and always at your best. These characteristics will separate you from the pack, because most people believe such a high level of achievement is unattainable. They are reluctant to stand out, feeling more comfortable conforming to societal norms of mediocrity. A person always striving for extraordinary, by contrast, accepts the opportunity to excel and shine.

Those who are always extraordinary are not looking to show off; they understand different can be extraordinary and can create progressive movement. People will immediately notice extraordinary individuals, and some will compliment you on this quality while others condemn you for it. Remember that you control your destiny.

*Extraordinary* is a mindset, an attitude, and an approach. You have the skills to activate these attributes to push yourself to greater things. Mercedes-Benz's slogan is "The best or nothing." To be the best, you must be extraordinary. I encourage you to promote yourself to extraordinary.

**R**
**E**
**F**
**L**
**E**
**C**
**T**
**I**
**V**
**E**

**P**
**A**
**U**
**S**
**E**

How are you going to be extraordinary?
Please list examples below:

_____

_____

_____

_____

_____

_____

_____

_____

_____

_____

_____

_____

_____

_____

_____

_____

_____

_____

An extraordinary effort can get
you to your mountaintop.

# nine

## GO BEYOND

## Go beyond . . .

To help others achieve
To raise your bar
To make your life count
To stay ready
To inspire
To think bigger
To be a product of your expectations
To change someone's emotional state
To believe before you see it
To surround yourself with positive people
To search for impact
To be extraordinary
To connect with others
To do more than what you get paid for
To value others
To get results
To fix problems

To "go beyond" means to do more than is expected or required. How do you go beyond in your life? Every day, I like to challenge myself to go beyond by leaving a deposit. A deposit is something positive that I do or say. It requires no money; just a nice gesture. That might mean opening a door for a stranger, appreciating teammates, smiling at someone, helping an elder, volunteering, donating items to Goodwill or the Salvation Army, mentoring, or being a role model for others. You know what your special talents are, so use them to "go beyond."

There were two gentlemen who were mid-level managers at the same company and unfortunately, due to downsizing, both were laid off. They each began looking for a new position, but they were repeatedly unsuccessful. After many months of rejections, one of the gentlemen quit looking for a job, stayed home, and complained to his friends and his wife about how unfairly he had been treated.

Meanwhile, the other gentleman kept looking for employment, even requesting to be a volunteer at the company that had most recently rejected him. The company agreed and reiterated that volunteers would receive neither salary nor benefits. The gentleman understood. He was the first one to arrive at work and the last one to leave. He worked hard to build professional relationships and always did his best. After a few months, a manager within the company unexpectedly resigned. Appreciating the volunteer's commitment, the company hired him to replace the manager. This distinguishes "go beyond" individuals from others. Are *you* willing to go beyond to make things happen in your life? There is winning and losing in life, but what is not acceptable is quitting. Be relentless and go beyond.

In what areas of life are you going
to push yourself to go beyond?
Please list examples below:

_____
_____
_____
_____
_____
_____
_____
_____
_____
_____
_____
_____
_____
_____
_____
_____
_____
_____

REFLECTIVE PAUSE

*Be careful how you toot your own horn. Be a product of your words by going beyond.*

# ten

## TIME

**It is time to . . .**

Thrust your life forward
Be creative
Read
Take baby steps
Believe
Laugh
Think
Complete those classes
Contribute
Change your attitude
Go higher
Become the person you want to be
Spend time with your family
Refresh your soul
Kiss the ones you love
Utilize your purpose
Make progress

Father time is undefeated. No one has ever beaten him, and we will never know how long we have left to live. Time can be neither bought nor sold; it can only be managed well, allowing us to increase our longevity and accomplish more in life.

Did you know that, in 2035, the World Time Society will add a 25th and 26th hour to our 24-hour day?

I am fibbing—I just wanted to get your attention. But here is a fun fact about time: If you were to place an atomic clock, which accurately measures time, in a high-elevation city, such as Denver, and another atomic clock in a low-elevation city, such as New Orleans, the atomic clock placed in the high-elevation city would record time more quickly as compared to the low-elevation city. Scientists say this is due to the weaker gravity present in higher elevations. Although the difference is only a matter of nanoseconds, one could say that people in higher elevations age slightly faster.

We all express concerns about not having enough time, or we feel that time is going by too fast. On average, human beings live for 78 years—which means 78 winters, 78 springs, 78 summers, and 78 falls. Given these terms, how can you create more time? First, cherish the moments that you are given: Cherish the minutes, the hours, the days, the weeks, the months, and the years you are blessed to be alive. Understand that these moments are either time that can be well-spent or time that can be taken for granted. When you focus on being more present, time seems to go by more slowly.

Second, take care of your body. It is a temple given to you by God. The food that you place in your mouth affects your body's health and wellbeing, warding off illnesses such as cancer, heart disease, diabetes, and inflammation. To extend your life by watching what you eat, I encourage you to research the world's five blue zones, one of which is in Loma Linda, California. Many people within these zones live beyond 100 years. Research the characteristics that add longevity to their lives, and note that a plant-based diet is one common characteristic of these communities. You should also monitor what you drink. You can choose soda, which has high-fructose corn syrup, making drinks taste sweeter and adding calories to your body, or you can consume a healthier alternative, such as alkaline water.

Third, keep your body active. To paraphrase Newton's first law of motion, a body at rest tends to stay at rest. Light strength training and four 30-minute cardio sessions per week are recommended, but you know your body best. Perhaps you might only do two 30-minute cardio sessions per week. Research healthy diets and workout routines to discover what works for you, BUT ensure that you have a plan. Your health choices can give you a longer life.

What are your objectives to extend your time?
Please list examples below:

_____

_____

_____

_____

_____

_____

_____

_____

_____

_____

_____

_____

_____

_____

_____

_____

_____

_____

R
E
F
L
E
C
T
I
V
E

P
A
U
S
E

Get out of the weeds and
stop wasting your valuable time.

# eleven

## GRATITUDE

## Gratitude is . . .

Giving
Maximizing opportunities
Thanking God for being able to
wake up each morning
Observing excellence
Service to others
Learning from lessons
Paying it forward
Vision
Having instinct
Receiving favor
Being there for others
Lending not borrowing
Life
Being able to love
Loving your children
Being a role model
Speaking to the world

Fred Rogers, aka Mister Rogers, offered these beautiful words during a university commencement: "From the time you were very little, you had people who have smiled you into smiling, people who have talked you into talking, people who have sung you into singing, people who have loved you into loving." In this same spirit, take a minute to think about someone who has helped you along the way, someone who has helped you get to this point in life, someone who has given you an opportunity to advance, someone who has motivated you with special words, or someone who lent you money to help you with a situation.

Some of these people might live down the street, some might be far away, and some might be in heaven. No matter where they are, deep down you know they always wanted what was best for you. They have always cared about you beyond measure and have encouraged you to realize and represent the best within you. Now, it is your turn to be an inspiration to others. How will you show your gratitude? Perhaps you could teach others to avoid those people who try to make them less than they are; perhaps you could teach others to not only improve their lives but to improve the lives of those around them; or, perhaps you could encourage individuals to embrace family life to the fullest.

It is your time to initiate gratitude. Pass it along to those who need it or who deserve it. It is easy to get caught up in yourself. Do not forget that there is much more to you. Make service to others a key attribute of your life. Be valuable. Be a completer. Give yourself no excuses. Make gratitude a part of your growth. Use your gifts to make everyone better. Tell yourself that you can do this.

REFLECTIVE PAUSE

How will you spread gratitude?
Please list examples below:

_____

_____

_____

_____

_____

_____

_____

_____

_____

_____

_____

_____

_____

_____

_____

_____

_____

_____

_____

What you appreciate. . .appreciates.
- Lynne Twist

# twelve

## EVOLVE

## To evolve is to . . .

Improve yourself
Be the "bigger person"
Change
Give credit to others
Accept input
Understand others
Embrace diversity
Be uncomfortable
Have a relationship with God
Bring joy to people
Put in a full-time effort
Have a growth mindset
Take pride in all that you do
Triumph over doubt and fear
Never give up
Make decisions that are unpopular
Practice integrity

Many people struggle to evolve in life; they resist developing, growing, changing, and progressing. You know how important it is to evolve, yet you fight it at times. In all aspects of your life, you must evolve: in relationships, in your education, in your career, in your parenting, and in your personal development. During your lifetime, your body changes, your spouse may change, your finances change, and your goals change. Evolving is inevitable. Take it on, enjoy it, and believe that things can only get better.

As discussed in the book *Change or Die*, surgeons who conducted heart bypass surgeries reported that 90% of their patients did not change their diets, smoking habits, or exercise routines for the better following their life-saving operations. It is amazing how we can refuse to evolve even when confronted with serious situations.

Here is an exercise that can help you evolve:

- ✓ When you hear the word *never*, think "now."
- ✓ When you hear the word *doubt*, think "do."
- ✓ When you hear the word *failure*, think "results."
- ✓ When you hear the word *cannot*, think "can."
- ✓ When you hear the word *maintain*, think "advance."
- ✓ When you hear the word *no*, think "yes" to new levels, new ideas, and new opportunities.
- ✓ When you hear the word *defeat*, think "determination."
- ✓ When you hear the word *trouble*, think "treasure."
- ✓ When you hear the word *worry*, think "worship."
- ✓ When you hear the word *passive*, think "pump it up."

Remember, everything starts in your thinking.

How are you going to evolve?
Please list examples below:

_____

_____

_____

_____

_____

_____

_____

_____

_____

_____

_____

_____

_____

_____

_____

_____

_____

_____

_____

_____

REFLECTIVE PAUSE

*Evolve by reading the signs
and taking the correct path.*

# thirteen

## GOLD MIND

## A gold mind is . . .

High expectations
A hunger for success
To create
Big ideas
To be in control of your environment
To reach for the stars
To refresh your soul daily
To pass along good energy
To be sharp at all times
To move beyond negativity
To be someone's rock
To motivate
To soar like an eagle
To reach new levels
To be determined
To love
To gain

The key to success is in the mind, the gold mind between your ears. One idea can make you healthy, wealthy, and wise. Ideas are free: You just need to devise them. Because of ideas, things get better every year—cars, cell phones, businesses, innovations, apps, and our lives, as just a few examples.

Do not do what everyone else is doing. There is a lot of mediocrity in the world—are you going to get stuck in it? It is easier to get comfortable on the couch than it is to push yourself to evolve. You are designed to create. You have genius in you that is waiting to come out. It is never too late to start. Consider that Henry Ford, founder of the Ford Motor Company, did not start his company until age 45.

Your attitude is an important part of your gold mind. If you feel you need to change your house, career, clothes, the people you associate with, your car, or anything else, you must first change your attitude. Your total environment is an exact reflection of you. If you spend countless hours practicing what you would like to accomplish, you will eventually achieve it. You will become that person. Everything takes effort; be determined to reach your goals. You will have to sacrifice to achieve. When your friend calls you to hang out, say, "No thank you, I'm in the middle of reaching my goals. I will catch up with you at a later time."

Those who are disciplined will realize their destiny. Those who understand success begins with conviction will realize their destiny. Those who are detailed will realize their destiny. Make up your mind to be "that" person. People earning big incomes made the decision that they wanted to earn more money. People who decide to invest, to be healthy, to overcome obstacles, to fight the good fight, or who simply want to be a positive force in life can do so. But only by having a gold mind.

R
E
F
L
E
C
T
I
V
E

P
A
U
S
E

What aspirations are inside your gold mind?
Please list examples below:

_____
_____
_____
_____
_____
_____
_____
_____
_____
_____
_____
_____
_____
_____
_____
_____
_____
_____

Never let the sun set on the
dreams in your mind.

# fourteen

## PATIENCE

## You can improve your patience by . . .

Being well-prepared
Taking a deep breath during high-stress situations
Having an attitude of: Everything will be just fine
Realizing that every day above
ground is a great day
Participating in activities that require patience
(e.g., chess, reading, or gardening)
Having a calm demeanor
Listening
Seeing things through the eyes of others
Focusing on the positives
Understanding people's personalities
Identifying what makes you impatient
Developing a plan to handle your impatience
Asking for help when you feel overwhelmed
Accepting what you cannot control
Exercising to reduce your stress
Accepting that your life will not be perfect
Remembering what really matters

What is the rush? Where is the fire? It seems that many people want a homerun these days. What is wrong with a single, double, or triple? Hurry and convenience have become the priorities in our go-go-go society. In relationships, we tend to move fast rather than getting to know people. If we are hungry, we pick up some fast food. If we have food at home, we often cook it in the microwave and—presto!—it is ready in a few minutes. If we want to purchase something, we order it online. It might even be delivered the same day. What happened to the "enjoyment" factor? Why do we not take the time to enjoy the day, the people, the events, and the general richness of life?

"Patience" is defined as the capacity to accept or tolerate delay, trouble, or suffering without getting upset. "Hmmm," many people would say, "good luck with that." However, if you are someone who struggles to be patient, you CAN change. A mantra that has inspired me throughout my life is: Go slow to go fast. I have implemented this notion in both my personal and professional lives. What does this expression mean? It means: Go slow at first—by reading, observing, asking questions, taking notes, researching, and shadowing others—and then practice the traits you have learned. You will find that, when you need to go fast in your parenting, leadership, or other endeavors, you will be prepared to move quickly.

You do not need to move fast all the time; "rush" mode stresses your body and leads to mistakes. Many people are in a hurry to fly the plane without first taking the time to move through the pre-flight checklist to ensure a safe and smooth journey. What do we all have in common? The answer is, life. Practicing patience can help you feel and see improvements in your life. Make it a habit to practice patience. When you become impatient—catch it and correct it.

How will you practice patience in your future?
Please list examples below:

_____

_____

_____

_____

_____

_____

_____

_____

_____

_____

_____

_____

_____

_____

_____

_____

_____

REFLECTIVE PAUSE

When the sun rises every day, everything will come to you at the right moment. Be patient.

# fifteen

## PREPARATION

## Preparation is . . .

An attitude
Necessary to excel
Success
Achievement
Effort
Self-confidence
An opportunity
Expecting results
A goal
Self-image
Excellence
Greatness
Thinking ahead
Being smart
Making the shift
Advancing

In life, your separation is your preparation. You cannot do most things without preparation. For example, imagine two brothers growing up in the same household. As they transition into adulthood, their lives could be totally different. One might have a great career, strong relationships, and a family life worth bragging about; the other might be in and out of prison, without career aspirations, and unable to avoid trouble. Why? It is because one brother was prepared to be successful, while the other brother did not prepare himself for success. The people you surround yourself with, the decisions you make, the relationships you build, the knowledge you gain, and the legacy you leave all depend on your preparation. Do you want to do great things in life? If so, then understand that preparation is essential.

Consider how much a player in the National Football League (NFL) must prepare. These athletes train in the spring, summer, and fall to play 16 or more games throughout the season. Football players spend significantly more time in practice than they do in games. There simply is no escaping the amount of preparation for NFL athletes; they must be disciplined, diligent, and dedicated.

People with excuses, people who are negative, people who have drama around them, and people who "can't get right" are people who do not prepare. The beautiful thing with preparation is, once you put in the time and demonstrate your commitment, everything becomes easier. Your self-confidence escalates, your presentation skills are sharpened, your words flow fluidly, people see purpose in you, and you have a spring in your step. As the saying goes, it is better to be prepared for an opportunity and to not receive it than it is to have an opportunity and not be prepared for it.

Everything is lined up for you. You hold the key to get in the car and transport yourself to "preparation city." The question is: Are you ready for the drive? Being unprepared means being unmotivated, unrewarded, unprofitable, and unsure. Create an attitude, even a culture, focused on preparation. Are you going to be average or awesome? Always be prepared to meet the moment. To reach maximum potential, be prepared to get out of your comfort zone.

How will you be more prepared in the future?
Please list examples below:

_____

_____

_____

_____

_____

_____

_____

_____

_____

_____

_____

_____

_____

_____

_____

_____

_____

_____

_____

_____

R
E
F
L
E
C
T
I
V
E
P
A
U
S
E

*Prepare to make a splash in
someone's life.*

# sixteen

## LEADERSHIP

## Leadership is . . .

Being a role model
Eating last
Going over and beyond
Setting the example
Working in the trenches
Standing out in a positive way
Arriving early and staying late
Being a visionary
Moving forward
Knowing your team
Being hungry for success
Working smarter than others
Following through
Valuing quality over quantity
Inspiring teammates to join you
rather than follow you
Getting knocked down but getting back up

Books often discuss varieties of leadership such as transformational, transactional, and authoritarian; but in my experience, the real distinction is between "seat leadership" and "feet leadership." Seat leadership means sitting in a seat to complete paperwork, answer emails, check voicemail messages, and correspond with staff members. Seat leaders rarely engage with their employees in-person, preferring to issue directives from their chairs. Anyone can be this type of leader; it requires only a minor amount of thinking as well as a minimal regard for teammates. Feet leadership, by contrast, means being down in the trenches with your team. This type of leadership entails completing work with your associates, walking around to gather information for decisions, motivating employees, asking for input, and having conversations that will move the team forward. Feet leaders are humanistic, courageous, empathetic, and motivated to benefit the entire team.

True leaders understand that, no matter how smart you are, if you do not know how to work with people, your goals are just goals. Leadership should never be taken for granted; it is a blessing to shape, mold, and guide others. It is an opportunity to inspire, transform, create a positive culture, and empower— to have the chance to turn nothing into something spectacular.

You are truly amazing. You get it! Now is your time to lead youngsters, to lead your organization, to lead seniors, to be a leader within your faith, to lead a business, to lead your learning, to lead your happiness, to lead your finances, to lead your relationships, and to lead leaders. Great leaders move others forward. Leaders ensure that, no matter the situation, hard work can solve problems. Leaders have something in them that causes them to stand out. Am I talking to you?

# R E F L E C T I V E   P A U S E

How can you use your
leadership to help others?
Please list examples below:

_____
_____
_____
_____
_____
_____
_____
_____
_____
_____
_____
_____
_____
_____
_____
_____
_____
_____

Use your leadership to create paths for others.

# seventeen

## INFLUENCE

## Influence is . . .

Powerful
Helping others
A gift
A positive act
Changing behaviors
Making an impact
Leadership
Modeling
An attitude
Exciting
Necessary
Success
Courage
Utilizing your purpose
Having people join you
A choice

As human beings, we have the same value; but our influence can differ. If you are the mayor of a town, for example, you can influence your constituents and the vision of your community. Likewise, as a parent, you can influence your children and their upbringing; as a professor, you can influence your students and their academic futures; and, as a doctor, you can influence your patients and their long-term health.

Reflect on how you can achieve the most influence in life. Once you have identified those areas, ask yourself this question: How can I maximize my influence? Know that influence is powerful. Your influence can steer someone down either the right or wrong path. Your influence could mean the difference between someone seeking help or not. Your influence could help someone get into college. Your influence could save a life.

Every year, challenge yourself to make a difference by using your influence. Focus on others; influence is not about you. You have been given a gift known as influence. Use it to be a hero. Believe me when I say, "The world needs more heroes." Influence has profound potential: Your words, talents, and skills have the power to make things happen for other people. Do not overthink things—just jump in and get started! You will be surprised by what your efforts can produce.

As Enaam Haddad put it, describing the power of influence: "My vision for a better Lebanon is when people really start to see and believe everyone has influence. Unfortunately, we only think of people in high positions as people of influence. But to see change in society, we need every man and women to know they have influence." Be the one to spread your influence; do something extraordinary with it.

How can you use your influence?
Please list examples below:

_____
_____
_____
_____
_____
_____
_____
_____
_____
_____
_____
_____
_____
_____
_____
_____
_____
_____

REFLECTIVE PAUSE

Use your influence to
help people cross bridges.

# eighteen

## FAITH

## Faith leads to . . .

Beautiful moments
Inspiring others
Expanding your territory
Fulfilling your purpose
Rising higher
Impacting the lives of others
God
Breakthroughs
Optimism
Quality
Happiness
Positive habits
Everything
Possibilities
Hope
Maturing

To have faith is to believe in something without evidence. Some people have faith that their children will grow up and make an impact in society. Others have faith that a higher power created the heavens and the earth. There are two types of people when it comes to faith: those who believe everything happens by chance and those who believe things happen because of a higher power. I am going to leave you with some wisdom on faith. You can agree with all of the information, you can agree with some of the information, or you can disregard the entire message. It is up to you. There is no right or wrong method for receiving this message.

The most important thing in life is to have a relationship with a higher power. This relationship does not necessarily mean you need to go to church every Sunday; it means you must follow the word of that higher power. Believe that your higher power has arranged your path. It knows your beginning and end, and it has placed and will keep gatekeepers along the way to assist you. Gatekeepers are people who will help you achieve your destiny. They can be either ordinary or influential people. Appreciate the people in your life, and accept guidance from them. Understand that receiving is not just for you; help others to receive by giving back.

What can you do to make an impact on someone's life, to help them move forward? We all rely on the help of others; the more you credit them, the more your higher power will bless you. We all have friends, coaches, mentors, and teachers who make us better. Your life is easier because someone has invested in you. You look good because of others, so do not take them for granted. Thank and appreciate them. Know that you are winning because of the faith others have in you.

**R E F L E C T I V E   P A U S E**

How will you use your faith
to improve your life?
Please list examples below:

_____
_____
_____
_____
_____
_____
_____
_____
_____
_____
_____
_____
_____
_____
_____
_____
_____

*Is your faith solid as a rock?*

# nineteen

## LOSS

**You can overcome loss by . . .**

Praying
Creating opportunities from it
Expecting it
Accepting it
Learning from it
Not letting it beat you down
Not getting stuck in it
Finding strength in it
Celebrating it appropriately
Facing it
Working toward happiness
Shifting your focus
Spending time with others
Allowing yourself time to heal
Keeping your faith
Controlling the fear of it

Why are people so fixed on winning in sports, winning over a spouse, winning the contract, winning the lottery, or winning at other opportunities? They are this way because so much of life is about imagining how you would like things to be. What we do not talk enough about, however, is loss. Is this because loss has a negative connotation? The obvious thing about loss is, as you age, you could lose many things, such as family members, pets, friends, or possessions. In addition, your financial situation could decline, your health could deteriorate, and you could even lose your livelihood.

Be aware that life is not always a straight line; things will happen, and loss is a part of that "happening." You often cannot avoid loss—but what you can do is to determine how you will handle it. At the end of your days, what will be your proof of life? Rise up every day whether you are winning or losing. When there is a loss in your life, make it a habit to get back up. Some people use loss as an excuse to stay down and out for the rest of their lives. Do not let that be you. Be the person who uses loss as an opportunity to advance yourself and others. You might, for example, donate the organs of a deceased loved one and thus give someone else a new lease on life.

According to Elisabeth Kubler-Ross, there are five stages of loss. They are: denial—denying the loss has occurred; anger—becoming angry with ourselves, others, or God over our loss, pain, and despair; bargaining—striking a deal with ourselves, others, or God to make the loss go away; depression—empty feelings present themselves on a deeper level; and acceptance—reaching a new level of understanding regarding the nature of our loss. Refuse to allow your heart and mind to get stuck in loss. Think about the opportunities you can develop from your losses.

How will you overcome losses in your life?
Please list examples below:

_____

_____

_____

_____

_____

_____

_____

_____

_____

_____

_____

_____

_____

_____

_____

_____

_____

_____

R
E
F
L
E
C
T
I
V
E

P
A
U
S
E

Be brave and prosper
from your losses.

# twenty

## IDENTITY

## Your identity is . . .

Bold
Positive
Forward-thinking
Reflective
Strategic
Capable of adding value to people
Different
Your attitude
The quality of your ideas
Your behavior
Earning your way
Zero excuses
Having a grander vision
Planting seeds
A presence every day
Your potential to have an impact

Identity is the qualities that make a person. Just when you think you have defined yourself, or life has defined you, there is always another chapter or challenge that will add to your identity and that may require you to leave your comfort zone. When you strive for something new, you will know what you are capable of.

Be careful with how you allow your past to define you. You can never escape the past, but you can always shape your future. You can control your identity while you move forward in life. Part of that control involves learning from past mistakes. Never let the naysayers, people who do not support you, or the haters shape your identity. If you want to have a positive identity, that is your choice. If you want to have a negative identity, that, too, is your choice. It may take years to create a positive identity, but it can take only seconds to destroy it. Crafting your identity means considering who you surround yourself with, managing how you think, and making good decisions about how you spend your time.

There is a concept called the law of the group that suggest that people who are likeminded tend to associate with one another. We see this in many aspects of our lives, such as in high school, where individuals stick within their groups: the athletes, the nerds, the drug users, the rockers, and so forth. Consider the people with which you surround yourself. They will influence you. Does that sound familiar? How are you thinking? Are your thoughts positive or negative? Can you talk over your negative thinking? You cannot have negative thoughts and still live a positive life. How do you spend your time? Are you productive, or do you waste your valuable time on things with no substance? Challenge yourself daily to add positive qualities to your identity. Keep it simple and realize this practice is making you a better person.

R
E
F
L
E
C
T
I
V
E

P
A
U
S
E

How will you develop your identity?
Please list examples below:

_____
_____
_____
_____
_____
_____
_____
_____
_____
_____
_____
_____
_____
_____
_____
_____
_____
_____
_____
_____

Is your identity making
positive waves?

# twenty-one

## LIFE

**Life is . . .**

Forgiving
Loving others
Going the extra mile
An expedition
Awesome
Joy
Keeping fear in check
Being a miracle for someone
Helping people change
Following your heart
Winning as the real you
Having a "can do" attitude
Leaving a positive legacy
Transforming from good to great
Learning and growing
Being thankful

Let us close this book with some final wisdom. Never forget how fragile life is: One day you are here, and the next day you could be gone. Because you are healthy and things are going well, you may fail to fully appreciate that life is short. Never believe that trials and tribulations are only for other people; you are not exempt from the bad and the ugly in life. Your mind might trick you into thinking that nothing bad will happen to you. Be aware of this thinking and always practice a life of gratitude. Life is about helping other people, bringing people together, fighting battles, practicing your faith, going through victories and defeats, and moving forward. If that is not life, what is?

One of the biggest challenges you will face in life is laziness. Why? Because being lazy is easier than stretching yourself to do the right things or to be different. Most people push the LAZY button because it is easier for them to just do nothing. This is why many people live an "Average Joe" life. Quit convincing yourself that you cannot do things. You are receiving this message on purpose. You can raise foster children, open up an animal shelter, reach your sales quota, find a spouse, travel the world, lead people, or make great decisions that will determine the stories you tell tomorrow.

You can reach new levels. You can set new standards. Be unusual. Grow yourself beyond what you are used to achieving. Enlarge your thinking. Realize that where you are is not your final destination. Be the person who tears down walls. Have an effect on others. Develop people. Live by the dream in your heart. Be a blessing. If you practice these characteristics, get ready for abundance in happiness, impact, and progress. This very moment, know that the right people are tracking you down.

How can you make an impact in life?
Please list examples below:

_____

_____

_____

_____

_____

_____

_____

_____

_____

_____

_____

_____

_____

_____

_____

_____

_____

_____

REFLECTIVE PAUSE

You "can't lose" if you. . .believe and go for it.

For more inspirational reading, check out my four
additional books (see below) available on Amazon.com

I also have inspirational videos on YouTube.
Type – Dr. Anthony J. Perkins to view.

# My Life Goal

I am dedicated to INSPIRING and spreading POSITIVITY by speaking to the world. I am interested in inspirational keynote speaking opportunities and personal development teaching opportunities for adults and students. If you wish to follow me on Facebook or YouTube, I can be found under: Dr. Anthony J. Perkins. You can write to me at: perkup67@yahoo.com. Thank you for your support. Be…an unrealistic thinker.

# About the Author

Dr. Anthony J. Perkins was born and raised in Connecticut but presently resides in Buckeye, Arizona. Dr. Perkins has served as an educational leader for almost three decades—as a teacher, vice-principal, principal, district director, and now school district superintendent. He holds a master's degree in education with an emphasis on diverse learners and a doctorate in educational leadership. In addition to his school experience, Dr. Perkins is a mentor for new school principals, and he teaches educational leadership classes (part-time) for Northern Arizona University. Dr. Perkins is the author of four additional books: *Make Leadership COUNT, Leadership: Wild, Wonderful, and Perfectly in Process, The Principle of Moments, and P3 Purpose - Pride - Progress.* Dr. Perkins' next adventure is inspirational speaking. He has started down this path and is seeking more opportunities to speak to the world. Dr. Perkins' interests include physical fitness, golf, and jazz music; however, he enjoys spending most of his time with his beautiful daughter.